White Paper Series

THE ENGLISH LANGUAGE IN THE DIGITAL AGE

Sophia Ananiadou University of Manchester
John McNaught University of Manchester
Paul Thompson University of Manchester

Georg Rehm, Hans Uszkoreit
(editors)

Editors
Georg Rehm
DFKI
Alt-Moabit 91c
Berlin 10559
Germany
e-mail: georg.rehm@dfki.de

Hans Uszkoreit
DFKI
Alt-Moabit 91c
Berlin 10559
Germany
e-mail: hans.uszkoreit@dfki.de

ISSN 2194-1416   ISSN 2194-1424   (electronic)
ISBN 978-3-642-30683-9 ISBN 978-3-642-30684-6   (eBook)
DOI 10.1007/978-3-642-30684-6
Springer Heidelberg New York Dordrecht London

Library of Congress Control Number: 2012940569

Printed on acid-free paper

Springer is part of Springer Science+Business Media (www.springer.com)

PREFACE

This white paper is part of a series that promotes knowledge about language technology and its potential. It addresses journalists, politicians, language communities, educators and others. The availability and use of language technology in Europe varies between languages. Consequently, the actions that are required to further support research and development of language technologies also differ. The required actions depend on many factors, such as the complexity of a given language and the size of its community.

META-NET, a Network of Excellence funded by the European Commission, has conducted an analysis of current language resources and technologies in this white paper series (p. 43). The analysis focusses on the 23 official European languages as well as other important national and regional languages in Europe. The results of this analysis suggest that there are tremendous deficits in technology support and significant research gaps for each language. The given detailed expert analysis and assessment of the current situation will help to maximise the impact of additional research.

As of November 2011, META-NET consists of 54 research centres in 33 European countries (p. 39). META-NET is working with stakeholders from economy (software companies, technology providers and users), government agencies, research organisations, non-governmental organisations, language communities and European universities. Together with these communities, META-NET is creating a common technology vision and strategic research agenda for multilingual Europe 2020.

META-NET – office@meta-net.eu – http://www.meta-net.eu

The development of this white paper has been funded by the Seventh Framework Programme and the ICT Policy Support Programme of the European Commission under the contracts T4ME (Grant Agreement 249119), CESAR (Grant Agreement 271022), METANET4U (Grant Agreement 270893) and META-NORD (Grant Agreement 270899).

The authors of this document are grateful to the authors of the White Paper on German for permission to re-use selected language-independent materials from their document [1]. Furthermore, the authors would like to thank Kevin B. Cohen (University of Colorado, USA), Yoshinobu Kano (National Institute of Informatics, Japan), Ioannis Korkotzelos (University of Manchester, UK), BalaKrishna Kolluru (University of Manchester, UK), Tayuka Matzuzaki (University of Tokyo, Japan), Chikashi Nobata (Yahoo Labs, USA), Naoaki Okazaki (Tohoku University, Japan), Martha Palmer (University of Colorado, USA), Sampo Pyysalo (University of Manchester, UK), Rafal Rak (University of Manchester, UK) and Yoshimasa Tsuruoka (University of Tokyo), for their contributions to this white paper.

TABLE OF CONTENTS

EXECUTIVE SUMMARY

In the space of two generations, much of Europe has become a distinct political and economic entity, yet culturally and linguistically Europe is still very diverse. While such diversity adds immeasurably to the rich fabric of life, it nevertheless throws up language barriers. From Portuguese to Polish and Italian to Icelandic, everyday communication between Europe's citizens, as well as communication in the spheres of business and politics, is inevitably hampered. To take one example, together, the EU institutions spend about a billion euros a year on maintaining their policy of multilingualism, i.e., on translation and interpreting services. Moreover, we tend to be shackled and blinkered by our linguistic environment, without, in many cases, being aware of this: we may be searching the Web for some piece of information and apparently fail to find it, but what if this information actually exists, is in fact findable, but just happens to be expressed in a different language to ours and one we do not speak? Much has been said about information overload, but here is a case of information overlook that is conditioned entirely by the language issue.

this otherwise insurmountable obstacle for the citizens of Europe and its economy, its capacity for political debate, and its social and scientific progress.

So, how can we alleviate the burden of coping with language barriers? Language technology incorporating the fruits of linguistic research can make a sizable contribution. Combined with intelligent devices and applications, language technology can help Europeans talk and do business with each other, even if they do not speak a common language.

However, given the Europe-wide scale of the problem, a strategic approach is called for. The solution is to build key enabling language technologies. These can then be embedded in applications, devices and services that support communication across language barriers in as transparent and flexible a way as possible. Such an approach offers European stakeholders tremendous advantages, not only within the common European market, but also in trade relations with non-European countries, especially emerging economies. These language technology solutions will eventually serve as an invisible but highly effective bridge between Europe's languages.

Language technology builds bridges.

Language technology is a key for the future.

One classic way of overcoming the language barrier is to learn foreign languages. However, the individual rapidly reaches the limits of such an approach when faced with the 23 official languages of the member states of the European Union and some 60 other European languages. We need to find other means to overcome

With around 375 million native speakers worldwide, English is estimated to be the third most spoken language in the world, coming behind only Mandarin Chinese and Spanish. Accordingly, since the dawn of work on language technology some 50 years ago, a large amount of effort has been focussed on the development of resources for English, resulting in a large number of high quality tools for tasks such as speech recognition and synthesis, spelling correction and grammar checking. Even today, the language technology landscape is dominated by English resources. Proof of this is evident just by looking at what has been going on in the research sphere: a quick scan of leading conferences and scientific journals for the period 2008-2010 reveals 971 publications on language technology for English, compared to 228 for Chinese and 80 for Spanish. Also, for automated translation, systems that translate from another language into English tend to be the most successful in terms of accuracy.

For many other languages, an enormous amount of research will be required to produce language technology applications that can perform at the same level as current applications for the English language. However, even for English, considerable effort is still needed to bring language technology to the desired level of a pervasive, ubiquitous and transparent technology. As the analysis provided in this report reveals, there is no area of language technology that can be considered to be a solved problem. Even if a large number of high quality software tools exist, problems of maintaining, extending or adapting them to deal with different domains or subjects remain largely unsolved. In addition, whilst the automatic detection of grammatical structure for English can already be carried out to quite a high degree of accuracy, the same cannot yet be said for deeper levels of semantic analysis, which will be required for next generation systems that are able to understand complete sentences or dialogues. In general, systems that can carry out robust, automated semantic analysis, e. g., to generate rich and relevant answers from an open-ended set of questions, are still in their infancy. However, some forerunners of these more intelligent systems are already available, which give a flavour of what is to come. These include IBM's supercomputer Watson, which was able

to defeat the US champion in the game of "Jeopardy", and Apple's mobile assistant Siri for the iPhone that can react to voice commands and answer questions.

Automated translation and speech processing tools currently available on the market also still fall short of what would be required to facilitate seamless communication between European citizens who speak different languages. On the face of it, free online tools, such as the Google Translate service, which is able to translate between 57 different languages, appear impressive. However, even for the best performing automatic translation systems (generally those whose target language is English), there is still often a large gap between the quality of the automatic output and what would be expected from an expert translator. In addition, the performance of systems that translate from English into another language is normally somewhat inferior.

The dominant actors in the field are primarily privately-owned for-profit enterprises based in Northern America. As early as the late 1970s, the European Commission realised the profound relevance of language technology as a driver of European unity, and began funding its first research projects, such as EUROTRA. In the UK, the then Department of Trade and Industry made a substantial co-investment to support UK EUROTRA participants. Many of today's language technology research centres in the EU exist due to the initial seed funding from that particular project. At the same time, national projects were set up that generated valuable results, but never led to a concerted European effort. In contrast to this highly selective funding effort, other multilingual societies such as India (22 official languages) and South Africa (11 official languages) have recently set up long-term national programmes for language research and technology development. The predominant actors in language technology today rely on imprecise statistical approaches that do not make use of deeper linguistic methods and knowledge. For example, sentences are often automatically translated by comparing each new sentence against thousands of sentences previously translated by humans, in an attempt to find a match, or a statistically close match. The quality of the output largely depends on the size and quality of the available translated data. While the automatic translation of simple sentences into languages with sufficient amounts of available reference data against which to match can achieve useful results, such shallow statistical methods are doomed to fail in the case of languages with a much smaller body of sample data or, more to the point, in the case of sentences with complex structures. Unfortunately, our complex social, business, legal and political interactions require concomitantly complex modes of linguistic expression.

Language Technology helps to unify Europe.

The European Commission therefore decided to fund projects such as EuroMatrix and EuroMatrixPlus (since 2006) and iTranslate4 (since 2010), which carry out basic and applied research, and generate resources for establishing high quality language technology solutions for all European languages. Building systems to analyse the deeper structural and meaning properties of languages is the only way forward if we want to build applications that perform well across the entire range of European languages.

European research in this area has already achieved a number of successes. For example, the translation services of the European Commission now use the MOSES open source machine translation software, which has been mainly developed through European re-search projects. In general, Europe has tended to pursue isolated research activities with a less pervasive impact on the market. However, the potential economic value of these activities can be seen in companies such as the UK-based SDL, which offers a range of language technologies, and has 60 offices in 35 different countries.

Drawing on the insights gained so far, it appears that today's "hybrid" language technology, which mixes deep processing with statistical methods, will help to bridge the significant gaps that exist with regard to the maturity of research and the state of practical usefulness of language technology solutions for different European languages. The assessment detailed in this report reveals that, although English-based systems are normally at the cutting edge of current research, there are still many hurdles to be overcome to allow English language technology to reach its full potential. However, the thriving language technology community that exists in English-speaking countries, both in Europe and worldwide, means that there are excellent prospects for further positive developments to be made. META-NET's long-term goal is to introduce high-quality language technology for all languages. The technology will help tear down existing barriers and build bridges between Europe's languages. This requires all stakeholders – in politics, research, business and society – to unite their efforts for the future.

This white paper series complements other strategic actions taken by META-NET (see the appendix for an overview). Up-to-date information such as the current version of the META-NET vision paper [2] and the Strategic Research Agenda (SRA) can be found on the META-NET web site: http://www.meta-net.eu.

LANGUAGES AT RISK: A CHALLENGE FOR LANGUAGE TECHNOLOGY

We are witnesses to a digital revolution that is dramatically impacting communication and society. Recent developments in information and communication technology are sometimes compared to Gutenberg's invention of the printing press. What can this analogy tell us about the future of the European information society and our languages in particular?

The digital revolution is comparable to Gutenberg's invention of the printing press.

Following Gutenberg's invention, real breakthroughs in communication were accomplished by efforts such as Luther's translation of the Bible into vernacular language. In subsequent centuries, cultural techniques have been developed to better handle language processing and knowledge exchange:

- the orthographic and grammatical standardisation of major languages enabled the rapid dissemination of new scientific and intellectual ideas;
- the development of official languages made it possible for citizens to communicate within certain (often political) boundaries;
- the teaching and translation of languages enabled exchanges across languages;
- the creation of editorial and bibliographic guidelines assured the quality of printed material;

- the creation of different media, like newspapers, radio, television, books and other formats, satisfied different communication needs.

Over the past twenty years, information technology has helped to automate and facilitate many of the processes, including the following:

- desktop publishing software has replaced typewriting and typesetting;
- Microsoft PowerPoint has replaced overhead projector transparencies;
- e-mail allows documents to be sent and received more quickly than using a fax machine;
- Skype offers cheap Internet phone calls and hosts virtual meetings;
- audio and video encoding formats make it easy to exchange multimedia content;
- web search engines provide keyword-based access;
- online services like Google Translate produce quick, approximate translations;
- social media platforms such as Facebook, Twitter and Google+ facilitate communication, collaboration and information sharing.

Although these tools and applications are helpful, they are not yet capable of supporting a fully-sustainable, multilingual European society in which information and goods can flow freely.

2.1 LANGUAGE BORDERS HOLD BACK THE EUROPEAN INFORMATION SOCIETY

We cannot predict exactly what the future information society will look like. However, there is a strong likelihood that the revolution in communication technology will bring together people who speak different languages in new ways. This is putting pressure both on individuals to learn new languages and especially on developers to create new technologies that will ensure mutual understanding and access to shareable knowledge. In the global economic and information space, there is increasing interaction between different languages, speakers and content, thanks to new types of media. The current popularity of social media (Wikipedia, Facebook, Twitter, Google+) is only the tip of the iceberg.

The global economy and information space confronts us with different languages, speakers and content.

Today, we can transmit gigabytes of text around the world in a few seconds before we recognise that it is in a language that we do not understand. According to a report from the European Commission, 57% of Internet users in Europe purchase goods and services in non-native languages; English is the most common foreign language, followed by French, German and Spanish. 55% of users read content in a foreign language, while 35% use another language to write e-mails or post comments on the Web [3]. A few years ago, English might have been the lingua franca of the Web – the vast majority of content on the Web was in English – but the situation has now drastically changed. The amount of online content in other European (as well as Asian and Middle Eastern) languages has exploded. Surprisingly, this ubiquitous digital divide caused by language borders has gained little public attention. However, it raises a very pressing question, i. e., which European languages will thrive in the networked information and knowledge society, and which are doomed to disappear?

2.2 OUR LANGUAGES AT RISK

While the printing press helped to further the exchange of information throughout Europe, it also led to the extinction of many languages. Regional and minority languages were rarely printed, and languages such as Cornish and Dalmatian were limited to oral forms of transmission, which in turn restricted their scope of use. Will the Internet have the same impact on our modern languages?

The variety of languages in Europe is one of its richest and most important cultural assets.

Europe's approximately 80 languages are one of our richest and most important cultural assets, and a vital part of this unique social model [4]. While languages such as English and Spanish are likely to survive in the emerging digital marketplace, many languages could become irrelevant in a networked society. This would weaken Europe's global standing, and run counter to the goal of ensuring equal participation for every citizen regardless of language. According to a UNESCO report on multilingualism, languages are an essential medium for the enjoyment of fundamental rights, such as political expression, education and participation in society [5].

2.3 LANGUAGE TECHNOLOGY IS A KEY ENABLING TECHNOLOGY

In the past, investments in language preservation focussed primarily on language education and translation. According to one estimate, the European market for translation, interpretation, software localisation and website globalisation was €8.4 billion in 2008 and is expected to grow by 10% per annum [6]. Yet, this figure covers just a small proportion of current and future needs for communication between languages. The most compelling solution for ensuring the breadth and depth of language usage in Europe tomorrow is to use appropriate technology, just as we use technology to solve our transport, energy and disability needs, amongst others. Language technology, targeting all forms of written text and spoken discourse, can help people to collaborate, conduct business, share knowledge and participate in social and political debate, regardless of language barriers and computer skills. It often operates invisibly inside complex software systems. Current examples of tasks in which language technology is employed "behind the scenes" include the following:

- finding information with a search engine;
- checking spelling and grammar with a word processor;
- viewing product recommendations in an online shop;
- following the spoken directions of an in-car navigation system;
- translating web pages via an online service.

Language technology consists of a number of core applications that enable processes within a larger application framework. The purpose of the META-NET language white papers is to focus on the state of these core technologies for each European language.

Europe needs robust and affordable language technology for all European languages.

To maintain its position at the forefront of global innovation, Europe will need robust and affordable language technology adapted to all European languages, that is tightly integrated within key software environments. Without language technology, it will not be possible to achieve an effective interactive, multimedia and multilingual user experience in the near future.

2.4 OPPORTUNITIES FOR LANGUAGE TECHNOLOGY

In the world of print, the technology breakthrough was the rapid duplication of an image of a text using a suitably powered printing press. Human beings had to do the hard work of looking up, assessing, translating and summarising knowledge. In terms of speech, we had to wait for Edison's invention before recording was possible – and again, his technology simply made analogue copies.

Language technology can now simplify and automate the processes of translation, content production and knowledge management for all European languages. It can also empower intuitive speech-based interfaces for household electronics, machinery, vehicles, computers and robots. Real-world commercial and industrial applications are still in the early stages of development, yet R&D achievements are creating a genuine window of opportunity. For example, machine translation is already reasonably accurate in specific domains, and experimental applications provide multilingual information and knowledge management, as well as content production, in many European languages.

As with most technologies, the first language applications, such as voice-based user interfaces and dialogue systems, were developed for specialised domains, and often exhibited limited performance. However, there are huge market opportunities in the education and entertainment industries for integrating language technologies into games, cultural heritage sites, edutainment packages, libraries, simulation environments and training programmes. Mobile information services, computer-assisted language learning software, eLearning environments, self-assessment tools and plagiarism detection software are just some of the application areas in which language technology can play an important role. The popularity of social media applications like Twitter and Facebook suggest a need for sophisticated language technologies that can monitor posts, summarise discussions, suggest opinion trends, detect emotional responses, identify copyright infringements or track misuse.

Language technology helps overcome the "disability" of linguistic diversity.

Language technology represents a tremendous opportunity for the European Union. It can help to address the complex issue of multilingualism in Europe – the fact that different languages coexist naturally in European businesses, organisations and schools. However, citizens need to communicate across the language borders of the European Common Market, and language technology can help overcome this barrier, while supporting the free and open use of individual languages. Looking even further ahead, innovative European multilingual language technology will provide a benchmark for our global partners when they begin to support their own multilingual communities. Language technology can be seen as a form of "assistive" technology that helps overcome the "disability" of linguistic diversity and makes language communities more accessible to each other. Finally, one active field of research is the use of language technology for rescue operations in disaster areas, where performance can be a matter of life and death: Future intelligent robots with cross-lingual language capabilities have the potential to save lives.

2.5 CHALLENGES FACING LANGUAGE TECHNOLOGY

Although language technology has made considerable progress in the last few years, the current pace of technological progress and product innovation is too slow. Widely-used technologies such as the spelling and grammar correctors in word processors are typically monolingual, and are only available for a handful of languages. Online machine translation services, although useful for quickly generating a reasonable approximation of a document's contents, are fraught with difficulties when highly accurate and complete translations are required. Due to the complexity of human language, modelling our tongues in software and testing them in the real world is a long, costly business that requires sustained funding commitments. Europe must therefore maintain its pioneering role in facing the technological challenges of a multiple-language community by inventing new methods to accelerate development right across the map. These could include both computational advances and techniques such as crowdsourcing.

The current pace of technological progress is too slow.

2.6 LANGUAGE ACQUISITION IN HUMANS AND MACHINES

To illustrate how computers handle language and why it is difficult to program them to process different tongues, let us look briefly at the way humans acquire first and second languages, and then examine how language technology systems work.

Humans acquire language skills in two different ways. Babies acquire a language by listening to the real interactions between their parents, siblings and other family members. From the age of about two, children produce their first words and short phrases. This is only possible because humans have a genetic disposition to imitate and then rationalise what they hear.

Learning a second language at an older age requires more cognitive effort, largely because the child is not immersed in a language community of native speakers. At school, foreign languages are usually acquired by learning grammatical structure, vocabulary and spelling, using drills that describe linguistic knowledge in terms of abstract rules, tables and examples. Learning a foreign language becomes more difficult as one gets older.

Humans acquire language skills in two different ways: learning by example and learning the underlying language rules.

Moving now to language technology, the two main types of systems acquire language capabilities in a similar manner. Statistical (or data-driven) approaches obtain linguistic knowledge from vast collections of example texts. Certain systems only require text in a single language as training data, e. g., a spell checker. However, parallel texts in two (or more) languages have to be available for training machine translation systems. The machine learning algorithm then learns patterns of how words, phrases and complete sentences are translated.

This statistical approach usually requires millions of sentences to boost performance quality. This is one reason why search engine providers are eager to collect as much written material as possible. Spelling correction in word processors, and services such as Google Search and Google Translate, all rely on statistical approaches. The great advantage of statistics is that the machine learns quickly in a continuous series of training cycles, even though quality can vary randomly.

The second approach to language technology, and to machine translation in particular, is to build rule-based systems. Experts in the fields of linguistics, computational linguistics and computer science first have to encode grammatical analyses (translation rules) and compile vocabulary lists (lexicons). This is very time consuming and labour intensive. Some of the leading rule-based machine translation systems have been under constant development for more than 20 years. The great advantage of rule-based systems is that experts have more detailed control over the language processing. This makes it possible to systematically correct mistakes in the software and give detailed feedback to the user, especially when rule-based systems are used for language learning. However, due to the high cost of this work, rule-based language technology has so far only been developed for a few major languages.

The two main types of language technology systems acquire language in a similar manner.

As the strengths and weaknesses of statistical and rule-based systems tend to be complementary, current research focusses on hybrid approaches that combine the two methodologies. However, these approaches have so far been less successful in industrial applications than in the research lab.

As we have seen in this chapter, many applications widely used in today's information society rely heavily on language technology. Due to its multilingual community, this is particularly true of Europe's economic and information space. Although language technology has made considerable progress in the last few years, there is still huge potential to improve upon the quality of language technology systems. In the next chapter, we describe the role of English in the European information society and assess the current state of language technology for the English language.

THE ENGLISH LANGUAGE IN THE EUROPEAN INFORMATION SOCIETY

3.1 GENERAL FACTS

Around the world, there are around 375 million native speakers of English. As such, it is estimated to be the third largest language, coming behind only Mandarin Chinese and Spanish. English is a (co)-official language in 53 countries worldwide.

Within Europe, English is the most commonly used language in the United Kingdom. It is not an official language in the UK, since there is no formal constitution. However, it can be considered the *de facto* language, given that it is the official language of the British government, and is spoken by around 94% of the 62 million inhabitants of the UK [7]. It is also the most widely spoken language in the Republic of Ireland (population approximately 4.5 million), where English is the second official language, after Irish. English is additionally the official language of Gibraltar (a British Overseas Territory) and a co-official language in Jersey, Guernsey and the Isle of Man (British Crown Dependencies), as well as in Malta. Outside of Europe, the countries with the greatest number of native English speakers are the United States of America (215 million speakers), Canada (17.5 million speakers) and Australia (15.5 million speakers).

In addition to English, the UK has further recognised regional languages, according to the European Charter for Regional or Minority Languages (ECRML), i. e., Welsh, Scottish Gaelic, Cornish, Irish, Scots, and its regional variant Ulster Scots. Since February 2011, the Welsh language (which is spoken by approximately 20% of the population of Wales) has shared official status with English in Wales [8]. The large number of British Asians (approximately 2.3 million or 4% of the population, according to the 2001 census) give rise to other languages being spoken in the UK, most notably Punjabi and Bengali.

English is a (co)-official language
in 53 countries worldwide.

Due to global spread of English, a large number of dialects have developed. Major dialects such as American English and Australian English can be split into a number of sub-dialects. In recent times, differences in grammar between the dialects have become relatively minor, with major variations being mainly limited to pronunciation and, to some extent, vocabulary, e. g., *bairn* (child) in northern England and Scotland. In addition to dialects, there are also a number of English-based pidgins and creole languages. Pidgins are simplified languages that develop as a means of communication between two or more groups that do not have a language in common. An example is Nigerian pidgin, which is a used as a *lingua franca* in Nigeria, where 521 languages have been identified. A creole language is a pidgin that has become nativised (i. e., learnt as a native language), such as Jamaican Patois. For further general reading on the English language, the reader is referred to [9, 10, 11, 12].

3.2 PARTICULARITIES OF THE ENGLISH LANGUAGE

Compared to most European languages, English has minimal inflection, with a lack of grammatical gender or adjectival agreement. Grammatical case marking has also largely been abandoned, with personal pronouns being a notable exception, where nominative case (*I*, *we*, etc.), accusative/dative case (*me*, *us*, etc.) and genitive case (*my*, *our*, etc.) are still distinguished.

A particular feature of the English language is its spelling system, which is notoriously difficult to master for non-native speakers. Whilst in many languages, there is a consistent set of rules that map spoken sounds to written forms, this is not the case in English. Nearly every sound can be spelt in more than one way, and conversely, most letters can be pronounced in multiple ways. Consequently, English has been described as "the world's worst spelled language" [13].

Consider the */u:/* sound, which in English can be spelt (among other ways) as "oo" as in *boot*, "u" as in *truth*, "ui" as in *fruit*, "o" as in *to*, "oe" as in *shoe*, "ou" as in *group*, "ough" as in *through* and "ew" as in *flew*. Having multiple written ways to represent a single sound is not in itself an unusual feature of written languages. For example, the same sound can be written in French as "ou", "ous", "out" or "oux". However, what is more unusual about English is the fact that most of the written forms have alternative pronunciations as well, e. g., *rub*, *build*, *go*, *toe*, *out*, *rough*, *sew*. One of the most notorious amongst the groups of letters listed is *ough*, which can be pronounced in up to ten different ways.

English has a notoriously difficult spelling system.

These special features of English are the result of a number of factors, including the complex history of the UK, which has been heavily influenced by previous invasions and occupations by Scandinavians and Normans. Also, the English spelling system does not reflect the significant changes in the pronunciation of the language that have occurred since the late fifteenth century. In contrast to many other languages, and despite numerous efforts, most efforts to reform English spelling have met with little success.

A further defining feature of English is the large number of phrasal verbs, which are combinations of verb and preposition and/or adverb. The meaning of phrasal verbs is often not easily predictable from their constituent parts, which make them an obstacle for learners of English. By means of an example, the verb "get" can occur in a number of phrasal verb constructions, such as *get by* (cope or survive), *get over* (recover from) and *get along* (be on good terms).

The meaning of English phrasal verbs is not easily predictable from their constituent parts.

3.3 RECENT DEVELOPMENTS

Events in the more recent history of the UK have had a significant influence on the vocabulary of English. These events include the industrial revolution, which necessitated the coining of new words for things and ideas that had not previously existed, and the British Empire. At its height, the empire covered one quarter of the earth's surface, and a large number of foreign words from the different countries entered the language. The increased spread of public education increased literacy, and, combined with the spread of public libraries in the 19th century, books (and therefore a standard language) were exposed to a far greater number of people. The migration of large numbers of people from many different countries to the United States of America also affected the development of American English.

The two world wars of the 20th century caused people from different backgrounds to be thrown together, and the increased social mobility that followed contributed to many regional differences in the language being lost, at least in the UK. With the introduction of radio broadcasting, and later of film and television, people were further exposed to unfamiliar accents and vocabulary, which also influenced the development of the language. Today, American English has a particularly strong influence on the development of British English, due to the USA's dominance in cinema, television, popular music, trade and technology (including the Internet).

The 20th century has seen the disappearance of many regional language differences in the UK.

The online edition of the Oxford English Dictionary is updated four times per year, with the March 2011 release including 175 new words, many of which indicate the rapidly changing nature of our society [14]. These words include initialisms such as *OMG* (Oh my god) and *LOL* (Laughing out loud), which reflect the increasing influence of electronic communications (e. g., email, text messaging, social networks, blogs, etc.) on everyday lives. An increasing thirst for travel and cuisines of the word has caused loan words such as *banh mi* (Vietnamese sandwich) to be listed.

The online Oxford English Dictionary is updated four times per year to accommodate the rapidly changing nature of the language.

Within Europe, English can today be considered the most commonly used language, with 51% of EU citizens speaking it either as a mother tongue or a foreign language, according to a EUROBAROMETER survey [15]. Considering non-native speakers of English in the EU, 38% state that they have sufficient English skills to hold a conversation. English is the most widely known language apart from the mother tongue in 19 of the 29 countries polled, with particularly high percentages of speakers in Sweden (89%), Malta (88%) and the Netherlands (87%).

51% of EU citizens speak English as another tongue or foreign language.

3.4 LANGUAGE CULTIVATION IN THE UK

There are a number of associations, both nationally and internationally, which aim to promote the English language. These include the English Association [16], which was founded in 1906, with the aims of furthering knowledge, understanding and enjoyment of the English language and its literature, and of fostering good practice in its teaching and learning at all levels. The Council for College and University English [17] and the National Association for the Teaching of English [18] promote standards of excellence in the teaching of English at different levels, from early years through to university studies. The European Society for the Study of English [19] promotes the study and understanding of English languages, literature and cultures of English-speaking people within Europe.

The Queen's English Society [20] (QES) is a charity founded in 1972, which aims to protect the English language from perceived declining standards. Its objectives include the education of the public in the correct and elegant usage of English, whilst discouraging the intrusion of anything detrimental to clarity or euphony. Such intrusions include the introduction of "foreign" words and, in recent years, words introduced through new technologies, such as internet chat and text messaging. As such, the aims of the QES appear to be in conflict with those of the Oxford English Dictionary, which aims to describe recent changes in the language, rather than taking a prescriptive view of what is correct. The aims of the QES are not so different from those of the language academies that exist in other European countries (e. g., L'Académie Française in France, the Real Academia Española in Spain and the Accademia della Crusca in Italy). These academies determine standards of acceptable grammar and vocabulary, as well as adapting to linguistic change by adding new words and updating the meanings of existing ones. Indeed, in 2010, it was attempted to form an Academy of English using a similar model to the academies listed above. However, such a prescriptive approach generated a large amount of bad press concerning objections to the suppression of linguistic diversity and evolution. Consequently, the project was abandoned after a few months.

3.5 LANGUAGE IN EDUCATION

From the early 1960s until 1988, there was little or no compulsory English grammar teaching in schools. The Education Reform act of 1988, and with it the introduction of the National Curriculum, has resulted in greater structure in the teaching of English in the UK, including the re-introduction of grammar as a required element. From ages 5-16, during which the study of English is a compulsory subject (except in Wales), the teaching requirements are divided into the key areas of listening, speaking, reading and writing [21]. The study of language structure, as well both standard English and variations (including dialects), together with culture, are an integral part of each of the key areas, and are developed throughout the learning process. Between 2003 and 2010, the study of a foreign language was only compulsory between the ages of 11-14, causing a 30% drop in the number of students opting to study a foreign language beyond 14. However, from 2010, foreign language learning was planned to begin at the age of 10.

From the age of 16, education in the UK is optional. A 2006 survey of subjects studied by 16-18 year olds in England found that English literature was the third most popular subject (after General Studies and Mathematics) [22], studied by approximately 19.5% of students. In contrast, only 7% per cent of students opt to study English language, making it the 14th most popular subject. This still puts it above the two most popular foreign languages, i. e., French at 22nd position (5% of students) and German at 29th position (2% of students). At degree level in UK universities, English ranked as the 6th most popular subject in 2010, with a small increase in applications (8.6%) compared to 2009.

The PISA studies [23] measure literary skills amongst teenagers in different countries. According to the results, UK students are failing to improve at the same rate as students in some other countries. Although the overall scores of UK teenagers have not altered significantly between 2000 and 2009, their performance compared to other participating countries has dropped from 7th to 25th position. According to the amount spent per student on teaching, the UK ranks 8th among the 65 countries taking part. The difference between the overall literacy score for the UK and the average score of all participant countries is not statistically significant, and as such, the UK has comparable rates of teenage literacy to countries such as France, Germany and Sweden and Poland. In the 2009 study, around 18% of UK students did not achieve the basic reading level.

In the PISA studies, a major factor influencing reading performance variability between schools was found to be the socio-economic background of the students. The UK has quite a large percentage of immigrant students, with around 200 different native languages being represented at British schools [7]. However, there is generally a small gap between the performance of natives and immigrants. Although immigrants who do not speak English at home have considerably reduced skills, children whose native language is not English receive linguistic support to enable them to attain the minimum level of understanding and expression to follow their studies. Within Europe, English is the most studied foreign language within schools, with a study carried out by Eurydice [24] revealing that 90% of all European pupils learn English at some stage of their education. It is the mandatory first foreign language in 13 countries of Europe.

90% of all European pupils learn English at some stage of their education.

3.6 INTERNATIONAL ASPECTS

Driven by both British imperialism and the ascension of the USA as a global superpower since the Second World War, English has been increasingly developing as the *lingua franca* of global communication. It is the dominant or even the required language of communications, science, information technology, business, aviation, entertainment, radio and diplomacy, and a working knowledge of English has become a requirement in a number of fields, occupations and professions, such as medicine and computing. As a consequence of this, over a billion people now speak English, at least to a basic level. Within the European Union, English is one of the three working languages of the European Commission (together with French and German). It is also one of the six official languages of the United Nations.

English has been increasingly developing as the *lingua franca* of global communication.

In science, the dominant nature of English can be viewed in two ways. On the one hand, its use as a common language in scientific publishing allows for ease of information storage and retrieval, and for knowledge advancement. On the other hand, English can be seen as something of a *Tyrannosaurus rex* – "a powerful carnivore gobbling up the other denizens of the academic linguistic grazing grounds" [25]. Scientists face a great deal of pressure to publish in visible (usually international) journals, most of which are now in the English language, leading to a self-perpetuating cycle in which English is becoming increasingly important.

The global spread of English is creating further negative impacts, e. g., the reduction of native linguistic diversity in many parts of the world. Its influence continues to play an important role in language attrition.

The global spread of English is reducing linguistic diversity in many parts of the world.

3.7 ENGLISH ON THE INTERNET

In 2010, 30.1 million adults in the UK (approximately 60%) used the Internet almost daily, which is almost double the estimate of 2006 [26]. The same report found that 19.1 million UK households (73%) had an Internet connection. It was found that Internet use is linked to various socio-economic and demographic indicators. For example, 60% of users aged 65 or over had never accessed the Internet, compared to 1% of those aged 16 to 24. Educational background also has an impact on Internet use. Some 97% of degree-educated adults had used the Internet, compared to 45% of people without formal qualifications.

In 2010, there were an estimated 536 million users of the English language Internet, constituting 27.3% of all Internet users [27]. This makes the English Internet the most used in the world – only the Chinese Internet comes anywhere close, with 445 million users. The third most popular language on the Internet is Spanish, with about 153 million users.

The English language internet is the most used in the world.

With 9.1 million registrations in February 2011, the UK's top-level country domain, *.uk*, is the fifth most popular extension in the world. It is also the second most used country-specific extension, beaten only by Germany's *.de* extension [28].

The growing importance of the Internet is critical for language technology in two ways. On the one hand, the large amount of digitally available language data represents a rich source for analysing the usage of natural language, in particular by collecting statistical information. On the other hand, the Internet offers a wide range of application areas that can be improved through the use of language technology.

With about 9 million Internet domains, the *.uk* extension is the world's second most popular country-specific extension.

The most commonly used web application is web search, which involves the automatic processing of language on multiple levels, as we will see in more detail in the next chapter. It involves sophisticated language technology, which differs for each language. For English, this may consist of matching spelling variations (e. g., British/American variations such as *colour/color*), or using context to distinguish whether the word *fly* refers to a noun (insect) or verb.

It is an expressed political aim in the UK and other European countries to ensure equal opportunities for everyone. In particular, the *Disability Discrimination Act*, which came into force in 1995, together with the more recent *Equality Act* of 2010, have made it a legal requirement for companies and organisations to ensure that their services and information are accessible to all. This requirement applies directly to websites and Internet services. User-friendly language technology tools offer the principal solution to satisfy this legal regulation, for example, by offering speech synthesis for the blind.

Internet users and providers of web content can also profit from language technology in less obvious ways, e. g., in the automatic translation of web contents from one language into another. Considering the high costs associated with manually translating these contents, it may be surprising how little usable language technology is built-in, compared to the anticipated need. However, it becomes less surprising if we consider the complexity of the English language, which has been partially highlighted above, and the number of technologies involved in typical language technology applications.

The UK's Equality Act of 2010 makes it a legal requirement for companies and organisations to make their websites and Internet services accessible to the disabled.

The next chapter presents an introduction to language technology and its core application areas, together with an evaluation of current language technology support for English.

4

LANGUAGE TECHNOLOGY SUPPORT FOR ENGLISH

Language technologies are software systems designed to handle human language and are therefore often called "human language technology". Human language comes in spoken and written forms. While speech is the oldest and, in terms of human evolution, the most natural form of language communication, complex information and most human knowledge is stored and transmitted through the written word. Speech and text technologies process or produce these different forms of language, using dictionaries, rules of grammar, and semantics. This means that language technology (LT) links language to various forms of knowledge, independently of the media (speech or text) in which it is expressed. Figure 1 illustrates the LT landscape.

When we communicate, we combine language with other modes of communication and information media – for example, speaking can involve gestures and facial expressions. Digital texts link to pictures and sounds. Movies may contain language in spoken and written form. In other words, speech and text technologies overlap and interact with other multimodal communication and multimedia technologies.

In this chapter, we will discuss the main application areas of language technology, i. e., language checking, web search, speech interaction and machine translation. These include applications and basic technologies such as the following:

- spelling correction
- authoring support
- computer-assisted language learning
- information retrieval
- information extraction
- text summarisation
- question answering
- speech recognition
- speech synthesis

Language technology is an established area of research with an extensive set of introductory literature. The interested reader is referred to the following references: [29, 30, 31, 32].

Before discussing the above application areas, we will briefly describe the architecture of a typical LT system.

4.1 APPLICATION ARCHITECTURES

Software applications for language processing typically consist of several components that mirror different aspects of language. While such applications tend to be very complex, figure 2 shows a highly simplified architecture of a typical text processing system. The first three modules handle the structure and meaning of the text input:

1. Pre-processing: cleans the data, analyses or removes formatting, detects the input languages, replaces "don't" with "do not" in English texts, and so on.

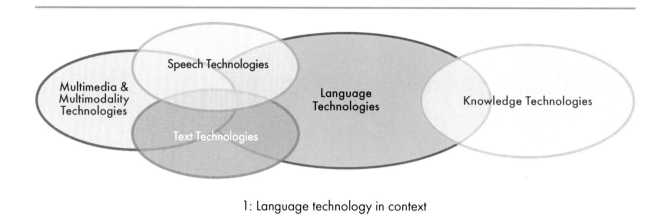

1: Language technology in context

2. Grammatical analysis: finds the verb, its objects, modifiers and other sentence elements; detects the sentence structure.

3. Semantic analysis: performs disambiguation (i. e., computes the appropriate meaning of words in a given context); resolves anaphora (i. e., which pronouns refer to which nouns in the sentence) and substitutes expressions; represents the meaning of the sentence in a machine-readable way.

After analysing the text, task-specific modules can perform other operations, such as automatic summarisation and database look-ups.

In the remainder of this chapter, we firstly introduce the core application areas for language technology, and follow this with a brief overview of the state of LT research and education today, and a description of past and present research programmes. Finally, we present an expert estimate of core LT tools and resources for English in terms of various dimensions such as availability, maturity and quality. The general state of LT for the English language is summarised in a matrix (figure 8 on p. 28). The matrix refers to the tools and resources that are emboldened in the main text of this chapter. LT support for English is also compared to other languages that are part of this series.

4.2 CORE APPLICATION AREAS

In this section, we focus on the most important LT tools and resources, and provide an overview of LT activities in the UK.

4.2.1 Language Checking

Anyone who has used a word processor such as Microsoft Word knows that it has a spell checker that high-

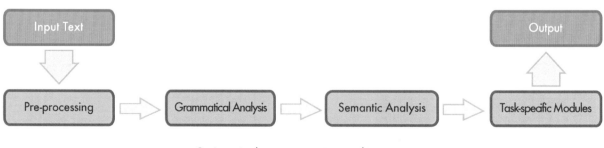

2: A typical text processing architecture

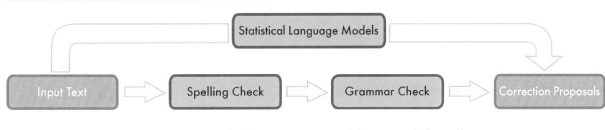

3: Language checking (top: statistical; bottom: rule-based)

lights spelling mistakes and proposes corrections. The first spelling correction programs compared a list of extracted words against a dictionary of correctly spelled words. Nowadays, these programs are far more sophisticated. Using language-dependent algorithms for **grammatical analysis**, they detect errors related to morphology (e. g., plural formation) as well as syntax–related errors, such as a missing verb or a conflict of verb-subject agreement (e. g., *she *write a letter*). However, most spell checkers will not find any errors in the following text [33]:

> I have a spelling checker,
> It came with my PC.
> It plane lee marks four my revue
> Miss steaks aye can knot sea.

Handling these kinds of errors usually requires an analysis of the context. This type of analysis either needs to draw on language-specific **grammars** labouriously coded into the software by experts, or on a statistical language model (see figure 3). In the latter case, a model calculates the probability that a particular word will occur in a specific position (e. g., between the words that precede and follow it). For example, *It plainly marks* is a much more probable word sequence than *It plane lee marks*. A statistical language model can be automatically created by using a large amount of (correct) language data, called a **text corpus**.

Language checking is not limited to word processors; it is also used in "authoring support systems", i. e., soft-

ware environments in which manuals and other documentation are written to special standards for complex IT, healthcare, engineering and other products. Fearing customer complaints about incorrect use and damage claims resulting from poorly understood instructions, companies are increasingly focussing on the quality of technical documentation, while at the same time targeting the international market (via translation or localisation). As a result, attempts have been made to develop a controlled, simplified technical English that makes it easier for native and non-native readers to understand the instructional text. An example is *ASD-STE100* [34], originally developed for aircraft maintenance manuals, but suitable for other technical manuals. This controlled language contains a fixed basic vocabulary of approximately 1000 words, together with rules for simplifying the sentence structures. Examples of these rules include using only approved meanings for words, as specified in the dictionary (to avoid ambiguity), not writing more than three nouns together, always using the active voice in instruction sentences, and ensuring that such sentences do not exceed a maximum length. Following such rules can make documentation easier to translate into other languages and can also improve the quality of results produced by MT software. The specification is maintained and kept up-to-date by the Simplified Technical English Maintenance Group (STEMG), which consists of members in several different European countries.

Advances in natural language processing have led to the development of authoring support software, which helps the writer of technical documentation use vocabulary and sentence structures that are consistent with industry rules and (corporate) terminology restrictions. The HyperSTE software [35], developed by Tedopres International, is such an example, which is based on the *ASD-STE100 specification*.

The use of language checking is not limited to word processors. It also applies to authoring support systems.

Besides spell checkers and authoring support, language checking is also important in the field of computer-assisted language learning. Language checking applications additionally automatically correct search engine queries, as found in Google's *Did you mean ...* suggestions.

4.2.2 Web Search

Searching the Web is probably the most widely used language technology application in use today, although it remains largely underdeveloped (see figure 4). The search engine Google, which started in 1998, is nowadays used for almost 93% of all search queries in the UK [36]. Since 2006, the verb *to google* has even had an entry in the Oxford English dictionary. The Google search interface and results page display has not significantly changed since the first version. However, in the current version, Google offers spelling correction for misspelled words and incorporates basic semantic search capabilities that can improve search accuracy by analysing the meaning of terms in a search query context [37]. The Google success story shows that a large volume of data and efficient indexing techniques can deliver satisfactory results using a statistical approach to language processing.

For more sophisticated information requests, it is essential to integrate deeper linguistic knowledge to facilitate text interpretation. Experiments using **lexical resources** such as machine-readable thesauri or ontological language resources (e. g., WordNet) have shown improvements by allowing pages to be found containing synonyms of the entered search term, e. g., the clever search engine [38]. For example, if the search term *nuclear power* is entered into this engine, the search will be expanded to locate also those pages containing the terms *atomic power, atomic energy* or *nuclear energy*. Even more loosely related terms may also be used.

The next generation of search engines will have to include much more sophisticated language technology.

The next generation of search engines will have to include much more sophisticated language technology, especially to deal with search queries consisting of a question or other sentence type rather than a list of keywords. For the query, *Give me a list of all companies that were taken over by other companies in the last five years*, a syntactic as well as a **semantic analysis** is required. The system also needs to provide an index to quickly retrieve relevant documents. A satisfactory answer will require syntactic parsing to analyse the grammatical structure of the sentence and determine that the user wants companies that have been acquired, rather than companies that have acquired other companies. For the expression *last five years*, the system needs to determine the relevant range of years, taking into account the present year. The query then needs to be matched against a huge amount of unstructured data to find the pieces of information that are relevant to the user's request. This process is called information retrieval, and involves searching and ranking relevant documents. To generate a list of companies, the system also needs to recognise that a particu-

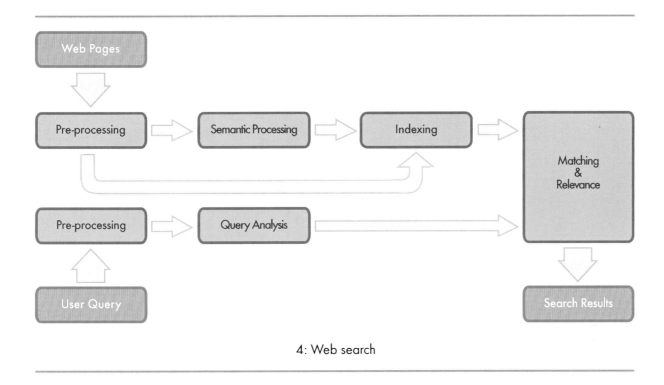

4: Web search

lar string of words in a document represents a company name, using a process called named entity recognition.

A more demanding challenge is matching a query in one language with documents in another language. Cross-lingual information retrieval involves automatically translating the query into all possible source languages and then translating the results back into the user's target language.

Now that data is increasingly found in non-textual formats, there is a need for services that deliver multimedia information retrieval by searching images, audio files and video data. In the case of audio and video files, a speech recognition module must convert the speech content into text (or into a phonetic representation) that can then be matched against a user query.

The first search engines for English appeared in 1993, with many having come and gone since those days. Today, apart from Google, the major players are Microsoft's Bing (accounting for approximately 4% of UK searches) and Yahoo (approximately 2% of searches in the UK, but also powered by Bing). All other engines account for less than 1% of searches. Some sites, such as Dogpile, provide access to meta-search engines, which fetch results from a range of different search engines. Other search engines focus on specialised topics and incorporate semantic search, an example being Yummly, which deals exclusively with recipes. Blinx is an example of a video search engine, which makes use of a combination of conceptual search, speech recognition and video analysis software to locate videos of interest to the user.

4.2.3 Speech Interaction

Speech interaction is one of many application areas that depend on speech technology, i. e., technologies for processing spoken language. Speech interaction technology is used to create interfaces that enable users to interact in spoken language instead of using a graphical display, keyboard and mouse. Today, these voice user interfaces (VUI) are used for partially or fully automated telephone services provided by companies to customers, employees or partners. Business domains that rely heavily on VUIs include banking, supply chain,

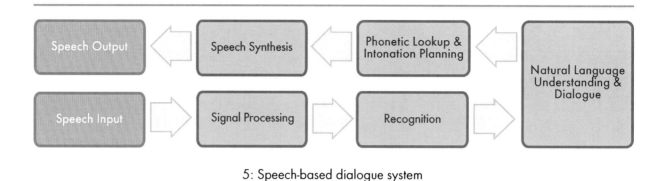

5: Speech-based dialogue system

public transportation and telecommunications. Other uses of speech interaction technology include interfaces to in-car satellite navigation systems and the use of spoken language as an alternative to the graphical or touchscreen interfaces in smartphones. Speech interaction technology comprises four technologies:

1. Automatic **speech recognition** (ASR) determines which words are actually spoken in a given sequence of sounds uttered by a user.

2. Natural language understanding analyses the syntactic structure of a user's utterance and interprets it according to the system in question.

3. Dialogue management determines which action to take, given the user input and system functionality.

4. **Speech synthesis** (text-to-speech or TTS) transforms the system's reply into sounds that the user can understand.

One of the major challenges of ASR systems is to accurately recognise the words that a user utters. This means restricting the range of possible user utterances to a limited set of keywords, or manually creating language models that cover a large range of natural language utterances. Using machine learning techniques, language models can also be generated automatically from **speech corpora**, i. e., large collections of speech audio files and text transcriptions. Restricting utterances usually forces people to use the voice user interface in a rigid way and

can damage user acceptance. However, the creation, tuning and maintenance of rich language models will significantly increase costs. VUIs that employ language models and initially allow a user to express their intent more flexibly – prompted by a *How may I help you?* greeting – are better accepted by users.

Companies tend to use utterances pre-recorded by professional speakers to generate the output of the voice user interface. For static utterances, where the wording does not depend on particular contexts of use or personal user data, this can deliver a rich user experience. However, more dynamic content in an utterance may suffer from unnatural intonation because different parts of audio files have simply been strung together. Through optimisation, today's TTS systems are getting better at producing natural-sounding dynamic utterances.

Speech interaction is the basis for interfaces that allow a user to interact with spoken language.

Interfaces in speech interaction have been considerably standardised during the last decade in terms of their various technological components. There has also been strong market consolidation in speech recognition and speech synthesis. The national markets in the G20 countries (economically resilient countries with high populations) have been dominated by just five global players, with Nuance (USA) and Loquendo (Italy) being the most prominent players in Europe. In 2011, Nuance announced the acquisition of Loquendo, which represents a further step in market consolidation.

On the UK TTS market, Google's interest in TTS technology has been demonstrated by their recent acquisition of Phonetic Arts [39], a company that already counted global giants such as Sony and EA Games amongst its clients. One of the selling points of Edinburgh-based CereProc is the provision of voices that have character and emotion. Roktalk is a screen reader to enhance accessibility of websites, whilst Ocean Blue Software, a digital television software provider, has recently developed a low-cost text-to-speech technology called "Talk TV", which has the aim of making the viewing of TV more accessible to those with visual impairment. The technology has been used to create the world's first accessible technology solution designed to provide speech/talk-based TV programming guides and set up menus. The Festival Speech Synthesis System [40] is free software that has been actively under development for several years by the University of Edinburgh, with both British and American voices, in addition to Spanish and Welsh capabilities.

Regarding dialogue management technology and know-how, markets are strongly dominated by national players, which are usually SMEs. Today's key players in the UK include Vicorp and Sabio. Rather than exclusively relying on a product business based on software licences, these companies have positioned themselves mostly as full-service providers that offer the creation of VUIs as a system integration service. In the area of speech interaction, there is as yet no real market for syntactic and semantic analysis-based core technologies.

Looking ahead, there will be significant changes, due to the spread of smartphones as a new platform for managing customer relationships, in addition to fixed telephones, the Internet and e-mail. This will also affect how speech interaction technology is used. In the long term, there will be fewer telephone-based VUIs, and spoken language apps will play a far more central role as a user-friendly input for smartphones. This will be largely driven by stepwise improvements in the accuracy of speaker-independent speech recognition via the speech dictation services already offered as centralised services to smartphone users.

4.2.4 Machine Translation

The idea of using digital computers to translate natural languages can be traced back to 1946 and was followed by substantial funding for research during the 1950s and again in the 1980s. Yet **machine translation** (MT) still cannot deliver on its initial promise of providing across-the-board automated translation.

At its most basic level, machine translation simply substitutes words in one natural language with words in another language.

The most basic approach to machine translation is the automatic replacement of words in a text written in one natural language with the equivalent words of another language. This can be useful in subject domains that have a very restricted, formulaic language, such as weather reports. However, in order to produce a good translation of less restricted texts, larger text units (phrases, sentences, or even whole passages) need to be matched to their closest counterparts in the target language. The major difficulty is that human language is ambiguous. Ambiguity creates challenges on multiple levels, such as word sense disambiguation at the lexical level (a *jaguar* is both a brand of car and an animal) or the attachment of prepositional phrases at the syntactic level:

- The policeman observed the man with the telescope.
- The policeman observed the man with the revolver.

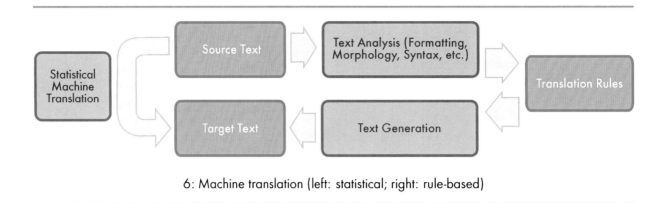

6: Machine translation (left: statistical; right: rule-based)

One way to build an MT system is to use linguistic rules. For translations between closely related languages, a translation using direct substitution may be feasible in cases such as the above example. However, rule-based (or linguistic knowledge-driven) systems often analyse the input text and create an intermediary symbolic representation from which the target language text can be generated. The success of these methods is highly dependent on the availability of extensive lexicons with morphological, syntactic and semantic information, and large sets of grammar rules carefully designed by skilled linguists. This is a very long and therefore costly process.

In the late 1980s, when computational power increased and became cheaper, interest in statistical models for machine translation began to grow. Statistical models are derived from analysing bilingual **text corpora**, called **parallel corpora**, such as the Europarl parallel corpus, which contains the proceedings of the European Parliament in 21 European languages. Given enough data, statistical MT works well enough to derive an approximate meaning of a foreign language text by processing parallel versions and finding plausible patterns of words. Unlike knowledge-driven systems, however, statistical (or data-driven) MT systems often generate ungrammatical output. Data-driven MT is advantageous because less human effort is required, and it can also cover special particularities of the language (e. g., idiomatic expressions)

that are often ignored in knowledge-driven systems.

The strengths and weaknesses of knowledge-driven and data-driven machine translation tend to be complementary, so that nowadays researchers focus on hybrid approaches that combine both methodologies. One such approach uses both knowledge-driven and data-driven systems, together with a selection module that decides on the best output for each sentence. However, results for sentences longer than, say, 12 words, will often be far from perfect. A more effective solution is to combine the best parts of each sentence from multiple outputs; this can be fairly complex, as corresponding parts of multiple alternatives are not always obvious and need to be aligned.

There are several research groups in the UK and the USA active in machine translation, both in academia and industry. These include the Natural Language and Information Processing Group of the University of Cambridge, the Statistical Machine Translation Group of the University of Edinburgh, the Center for Machine Translation at the Carnegie Mellon University and the Natural Language Processing groups at both Microsoft Research and IBM Research.

SYSTRAN is one of the oldest machine translation companies, founded in 1968 in the USA and having carried out extensive work for the United States Department of Defense and the European Commission. The current version of their software uses hybrid technology and offers capabilities to translate between 52 different languages. SYSTRAN is used to provide translation services on the Internet portals Yahoo, Lycos and AltaVista. Although Google originally also made use of SYSTRAN's services, they now use their own statistical-based system, which supports 57 different languages. Microsoft uses their own syntax-based statistical machine translation technology to provide translation services within their Bing search engine.

In the UK, automated translation solutions are provided by companies such as SDL, who makes available a free web-based translation service in addition to commercial products. Very specialised MT systems have also been developed, e. g., the LinguaNet system, created by Cambridge-based Prolingua. This is a specially designed messaging system for cross-border, mission critical operational communication by police, fire, ambulance, medical, coastguard, disaster response coordinators. It is currently used by 50 police sites in Belgium, France, the Netherlands, Spain, United Kingdom, Denmark, and Germany.

There is still huge potential for improving the quality of MT systems. The challenges involve adapting language resources to a given subject domain or user area, and integrating the technology into workflows that already have term bases and translation memories. Evaluation campaigns help to compare the quality of MT systems, their approaches and the status of the systems for different language pairs. Figure 7, which was prepared during the Euromatrix+ project, shows the pair-wise performances obtained for 22 of the 23 EU languages (Irish was not compared). The results are ranked according to a BLEU score, which increases according to the quality of the translation [42]. A human translator would normally expect to achieve around 80 points. The best results (in green and blue) were achieved by languages that benefit from a considerable research effort in coordinated programmes and the existence of many parallel corpora (e. g., English, French, Dutch, Spanish and German). The languages with poorer results are shown in red. These either lack such development efforts or are structurally very different from other languages (e. g., Hungarian, Maltese, Finnish).

4.3 OTHER APPLICATION AREAS

Building language technology applications involves a range of subtasks that do not always surface at the level of interaction with the user, but they provide significant service functionalities "behind the scenes" of the system in question. They all form important research issues that have now evolved into individual sub-disciplines of computational linguistics.

Question answering, for example, is an active area of research for which annotated corpora have been built and scientific competitions have been initiated. The concept of question answering goes beyond keyword-based searches (in which the search engine responds by delivering a collection of potentially relevant documents) and by enabling users to ask a concrete question, to which the system provides a single answer. For example:

Question: How old was Neil Armstrong when he stepped on the moon?

Answer: 38.

While question answering is obviously related to the core area of web search, it is nowadays an umbrella term for such research issues as: which different types of questions exist, and how they should be handled; how a set of documents that potentially contain the answer can be analysed and compared (do they provide conflicting answers?); and how specific information (the answer) can be reliably extracted from a document without ignoring the context. Question answering is in turn related to information extraction (IE), an area that was extremely popular and influential when computational

										Target language										
	EN	BG	DE	CS	DA	EL	ES	ET	FI	FR	HU	IT	LT	LV	MT	NL	PL	PT	RO	SK	SL	SV
EN	–	40.5	46.8	52.6	50.0	41.0	55.2	34.8	38.6	50.1	37.2	50.4	39.6	43.4	39.8	52.3	49.2	55.0	49.0	44.7	50.7	52.0
BG	61.3	–	38.7	39.4	39.6	34.5	46.9	25.5	26.7	42.4	22.0	43.5	29.3	29.1	25.9	44.9	35.1	45.9	36.8	34.1	34.1	39.9
DE	53.6	26.3	–	35.4	43.1	32.8	47.1	26.7	29.5	39.4	27.6	42.7	27.6	30.3	19.8	50.2	30.2	44.1	30.7	29.4	31.4	41.2
CS	58.4	32.0	42.6	–	43.6	34.6	48.9	30.7	30.5	41.6	27.4	44.3	34.5	35.8	26.3	46.5	39.2	45.7	36.5	43.6	41.3	42.9
DA	57.6	28.7	44.1	35.7	–	34.3	47.5	27.8	31.6	41.3	24.2	43.8	29.7	32.9	21.1	48.5	34.3	45.4	33.9	33.0	36.2	47.2
EL	59.5	32.4	43.1	37.7	44.5	–	54.0	26.5	29.0	48.3	23.7	49.6	29.0	32.6	23.8	48.9	34.2	52.5	37.2	33.1	36.3	43.3
ES	60.0	31.1	42.7	37.5	44.4	39.4	–	25.4	28.5	51.3	24.0	51.7	26.8	30.5	24.6	48.8	33.9	57.3	38.1	31.7	33.9	43.7
ET	52.0	24.6	37.3	35.2	37.8	28.2	40.4	–	37.7	33.4	30.9	37.0	35.0	36.9	20.5	41.3	32.0	37.8	28.0	30.6	32.9	37.3
FI	49.3	23.2	36.0	32.0	37.9	27.2	39.7	34.9	–	29.5	27.2	36.6	30.5	32.5	19.4	40.6	28.8	37.5	26.5	27.3	28.2	37.6
FR	64.0	34.5	45.1	39.5	47.4	42.8	60.9	26.7	30.0	–	25.5	56.1	28.3	31.9	25.3	51.6	35.7	61.0	43.8	33.1	35.6	45.8
HU	48.0	24.7	34.3	30.0	33.0	25.5	34.1	29.6	29.4	30.7	–	33.5	29.6	31.9	18.1	36.1	29.8	34.2	25.7	25.6	28.2	30.5
IT	61.0	32.1	44.3	38.9	45.8	40.6	26.9	25.0	29.7	52.7	24.2	–	29.4	32.6	24.6	50.5	35.2	56.5	39.3	32.5	34.7	44.3
LT	51.8	27.6	33.9	37.0	36.8	26.5	21.1	34.2	32.0	34.4	28.5	36.8	–	40.1	22.2	38.1	31.6	31.6	29.3	31.8	35.3	35.3
LV	54.0	29.1	35.0	37.8	38.5	29.7	8.0	34.2	32.4	35.6	29.3	38.9	38.4	–	23.3	41.5	34.4	39.6	31.0	33.3	37.1	38.0
MT	72.1	32.2	37.2	37.9	38.9	33.7	48.7	26.9	25.8	42.4	22.4	43.7	30.2	33.2	–	44.0	37.1	45.9	38.9	35.8	40.0	41.6
NL	56.9	29.3	46.9	37.0	45.4	35.3	49.7	27.5	29.8	43.4	25.3	44.5	28.6	31.7	22.0	–	32.0	47.7	33.0	30.1	34.6	43.6
PL	60.8	31.5	40.2	44.2	42.1	34.2	46.2	29.2	29.0	40.0	24.5	43.2	33.2	35.6	27.9	44.8	–	44.1	38.2	38.2	39.8	42.1
PT	60.7	31.4	42.9	38.4	42.8	40.2	60.7	26.4	29.2	53.2	23.8	52.8	28.0	31.5	24.8	49.3	34.5	–	39.4	32.1	34.4	43.9
RO	60.8	33.1	38.5	37.8	40.3	35.6	50.4	24.6	26.2	46.5	25.0	44.8	28.4	29.9	28.7	43.0	35.8	48.5	–	31.5	35.1	39.4
SK	60.8	32.6	39.4	48.1	41.0	33.3	46.2	29.8	28.4	39.4	27.4	41.8	33.8	36.7	28.5	44.4	39.0	43.3	35.3	–	42.6	41.8
SL	61.0	33.1	37.9	43.5	42.6	34.0	47.0	31.1	28.8	38.2	25.7	42.3	34.6	37.3	30.0	45.9	38.2	44.1	35.8	38.9	–	42.7
SV	58.5	26.9	41.0	35.6	46.6	33.3	46.6	27.4	30.9	38.9	22.7	42.0	28.2	31.0	23.7	45.6	32.2	44.2	32.7	31.3	33.5	–

7: Machine translation between 22 EU-languages [41]

linguistics took a statistical turn in the early 1990s. IE aims to identify specific pieces of information in specific classes of documents, such as the key players in company takeovers as reported in newspaper stories. Another common scenario that has been studied is reports on terrorist incidents. The task here consists of mapping appropriate parts of the text to a template that specifies the perpetrator, target, time, location and results of the incident. Domain-specific template-filling is the central characteristic of IE, which makes it another example of a "behind the scenes" technology that forms a well-demarcated research area, which in practice needs to be embedded into a suitable application environment.

Language technology applications often provide significant service functionalities behind the scenes of larger software systems.

Text summarisation and **text generation** are two borderline areas that can act either as standalone applications or play a supporting role. Summarisation attempts to give the essentials of a long text in a short form, and is one of the features available in Microsoft Word. It uses a mostly statistical approach to identify the "important" words in a text (i. e., words that occur very frequently in the text in question but less frequently in general language use) and determine which sentences contain the most of these important words. These sentences are then extracted and combined together to create the summary. In this very common commercial scenario, summarisation is simply a form of sentence extraction, in which the text is reduced to a subset of its sentences. An alternative approach, for which some research has been carried out, is to generate brand new sentences that do not exist in the source text. This requires a deeper understanding of the text, which means that, currently, this approach is far less robust. On the whole, a text generator is rarely used as a stand-alone application, but rather is embedded into a larger software environment, such as a clinical information system that collects, stores and processes patient data. Creating reports is just one of many applications for text summarisation.

For English, question answering, information extraction and summarisation have been the subject of numerous open competitions since the 1990s, primarily organised by DARPA/NIST in the United States, which have significantly improved the state of the art. For example, the annual TREC (Text REtrieval Conference) series included a question-answering track between 1999 and 2007. Recently, freely accessible tools have been developed that reason and compute answers. These include True Knowledge, developed in the UK, and Wolfram Alpha, developed in the USA. Question-answering systems in more specialist domains have also begun to emerge, such as the EAGLi system for questions answering in the Genomics literature, developed at the University of Applied Sciences, Geneva.

Information Extraction research for English was boosted by both the series of MUCs (Message Understanding Conferences), running from 1987 to 1998, and subsequently by the Automatic Content Extraction (ACE) program, running from 1999 to 2008. Domain-specific challenges such as BioCreAtIvE (Critical Assessment of Information Extraction systems in Biology), of which the most recent was held in 2010, have helped to further research into Information Extraction from more specialised types of text. Evaluation of text summarisation systems was carried out as part of the Document Understanding Conferences (DUC) from 2001 to 2007, and more recently as one of the tracks in the Text Analysis Conferences (TAC). Web-based tools such as Ultimate Research Assistant and iResearch Reporter can produce summary reports of retrieved search results.

4.4 EDUCATIONAL PROGRAMMES

In the UK, a large number of universities have well-established research groups that are active in the field of language technology or computational linguistics. These are complemented by many other groups in English speaking countries, most notably the USA, Australia and Ireland. These groups are most often part of either computer science or linguistics departments. The University of Manchester hosts the National Centre for Text Mining (NaCTeM), which is the world's first publicly funded text mining centre, providing text mining services to both academic institutions and industrial organisations. Over the past few years, there has been an increasing interest in tools and resources dealing with specialist domains such as biomedicine, molecular biology and chemistry.

In terms of teaching in the UK, courses with a large element of natural language processing or computational linguistics are rare, and are normally only offered at the masters level. Examples include the MSc in Speech and Language Processing and the MSc in Cognitive Science, offered at the University of Edinburgh. A greater number of universities offer course modules in NLP to students of more general degree programs. Examples include Birmingham, Cambridge, Manchester and Leeds.

4.5 NATIONAL PROJECTS AND INITIATIVES

The first working demonstration of an LT system took place in the 1950s. This system constituted a Russian–English Machine Translation (MT) system, developed by IBM and Georgetown University.

The company SYSTRAN, which was founded in 1968, had the original aim of processing the same language pair for the United States Airforce. SYSTRAN still exists today, as described in the *Machine translation* section above.

An early LT programme, EUROTRA, was an ambitious Machine Translation (MT) project inspired by the modest success of SYSTRAN, and established and funded by the European Commission from the late 1970s until 1994. The project was motivated by one of the founding principles of the EU: that all citizens had the right to read any and all proceedings of the Commission in their own language. A large network of European computational linguists embarked upon the EUROTRA project with the hope of creating a state-of-the-art MT system for the then seven, later nine, official languages of the European Community. However, as time passed, expectations became tempered; "Fully Automatic High Quality Translation" was not a reasonably attainable goal. The true character of EUROTRA was eventually acknowledged to be pre-competitive research, rather than prototype development. While EUROTRA never delivered a working MT system, the project made a far-reaching long-term impact on the nascent language industries in European member states.

The Alvey Programme was the dominating focus of Information Technology research in the UK between 1983 and 1988. Amongst the areas of interest was Man Machine Interaction. The programme funded three projects at the Universities of Cambridge, Edinburgh and Lancaster to provide tools for use in natural language processing research. The tools, i. e., a morphological analyser, parsers, a grammar and lexicon were usable individually as well as together – integrated by a grammar development environment – forming a complete system for the morphological, syntactic and semantic analysis of a considerable subset of English.

The creation of the British National Corpus (BNC) was a major project that took place between 1991 and 1994. The corpus constitutes a 100 million word collection of samples of written and spoken language from a wide range of sources, designed to represent a broad cross-section of British English from the later part of the 20th century. The corpus is encoded according to the Guidelines of the Text Encoding Initiative (TEI) to represent both the output from CLAWS (automatic part-of-speech tagger) and a variety of other structural properties of texts (e. g., headings, paragraphs, lists etc.). An XML version of the corpus was released in 2007. Corpora of other varieties of English are also being collected. The International Corpus of English (ICE), whose collection began in 1990, involves 23 research teams around the world, who are preparing electronic corpora of their own national or regional variety of English. Each team is producing a corpus consisting of one million words of spoken and written English produced after 1989. The Corpus of Contemporary American English (COCA) consists of 425 million words, equally divided among spoken, fiction, popular magazines, newspapers and academic texts, consisting of 20 million words each year from 1990 to 2011.

AKT (2000-2007), was a multi-million pound collaboration between five UK universities, with the aim of enhancing information and knowledge management in the age of the World Wide Web. The team of 119 staff was interdisciplinary, involving leading figures in the worlds of multimedia, natural language processing and computational linguistics, agents, artificial intelligence, formal methods, machine learning and e-science. The research conducted on the project formed an important contribution to the semantic web, in which the use of LT played a central role. The AKT collaboration was a significant success in terms of papers published, grants awarded (36 other projects), students trained and international impact. It was rated as "outstanding" by the review panel. The collaboration placed major importance on making links with industrial partners, and finally it led to the founding of a number of spin-off companies. A follow-up project, "EnAKTing the Unbounded

Data Web: Challenges in Web Science", ended in March 2012.

Since many LT applications make use of similar sets of processing components, such as tokenisers, taggers, parsers, named entity recognisers, etc., the speed with which new applications can be developed can be greatly increased if such processing components can be reused and repurposed in flexible ways to create a range of different LT applications. Two systems which support the user in creating new applications from existing libraries of processing components are the University of Sheffield's GATE system, which has been under development for over 15 years, and the more recent U-Compare system, which was developed as part of a collaboration between the Universities of Tokyo, Manchester and Colorado. Whilst current components in U-Compare mainly deal with English, the library will be extended as part of META-NET to cover a number of different European languages.

As we have seen, previous programmes have led to the development of a large number of LT tools and resources for the English language. In the following section, the current state of LT support for English is summarised.

4.6 AVAILABILITY OF TOOLS AND RESOURCES

Figure 8 provides a general picture of the current state of language technology support for the English language. This rating of existing tools and resources was generated by leading experts in the field who provided estimates based on a scale from 0 (very low) to 6 (very high) using seven different criteria. For English, key results regarding technologies and resources include the following:

- No single category of technology or resources has consistently high scores across all criteria being evaluated.

- Generally, quantity, quality and availability can only be guaranteed for tools and resources dealing with more basic levels of linguistic processing.

- Higher levels of linguistic processing still present considerable challenges. The lower number of corpora annotated with these levels of information could be a factor limiting the advancement of these technologies, since the development of such technologies is more difficult if the amount of data on which they can be trained is limited.

- In general, speech processing technology is better developed than text processing technology. Indeed, speech technology has already been integrated into many everyday applications, from spoken dialogue systems and voice-based interfaces to mobile phones and in-car satellite navigation systems.

- Sustainability is, in general, a major area of concern. Even if high quality technologies and resources exist, major efforts may still be required to ensure that they are kept up-to-date and can easily be integrated into other systems. There is also often a lack of rigorous software testing/engineering principles applied to tools. The availability of the high-performance Lucene search engine for Information Retrieval, and the high quality test suites for grammar engineering, make these two areas notable exceptions.

- In general, tools that work well on a particular type of text may require considerable work to allow them to be applied to new text domains. Resources such as annotated corpora are also normally domain-specific, and creating these corpora for new domains generally requires a large amount of manual work.

- For all technologies and tools, there are examples that are available free of charge. However, the number of such tools and resources varies greatly according to category. In some cases, quality comes at a price. For example, in the case of syntactic corpora, there is little to rival the Penn TreeBank, which is

	Quantity	Availability	Quality	Coverage	Maturity	Sustainability	Adaptability
Language Technology: Tools, Technologies and Applications							
Speech Recognition	5	3	5	5	4	2	3
Speech Synthesis	5	3	4.5	5.5	4	2	3
Grammatical analysis	5	5	5.5	4.5	4.5	3	4
Semantic analysis	3	2	3	3	2.5	2	2
Text generation	3	3	3.5	2.5	2.5	2	2.5
Machine translation	4	4	3.5	4	4	2	2
Language Resources: Resources, Data and Knowledge Bases							
Text corpora	5	4	5.5	4	5	2.5	4
Speech corpora	5	2	6	5.5	5	3	3
Parallel corpora	4.5	4.5	5	5	3.5	3	3
Lexical resources	4	6	5	5	4.5	4.5	4.5
Grammars	3.5	2.5	4	4	2.5	4	1.5

8: State of language technology support for English

only available for a fee. In other cases, even large corpora are available free of charge, e. g., Google's n-gram corpus for statistical language modelling, which was created from 1 trillion word tokens of text from publicly accessible Web pages.

- Some broad areas, such as semantic analysis, consist of a number of component technologies. Whilst some of these technologies (e. g., named entity tagging), are quite mature and can produce high quality results, others, such as event/relation extraction are more complex and still require improvement. The scores awarded attempt to balance the different stages of development of these technologies.

- The current legal situation restricts making use of digital texts for empirical linguistic and language technology research, for example, to train statistical language models. However, a recent review by Professor Ian Hargreaves represents a step forward towards an Intellectual Property regime which is suited to the needs of 21st century business and consumers. Implementation of the proposals would allow copyrighted texts that have been legally acquired/bought/subscribed to, to be used by researchers for language-related R&D activities. The UK Government has accepted the proposals and is currently consulting on implementation.

- The cooperation between the Language Technology community and those involved with the Semantic Web and the closely related Linked Open Data movement should be intensified, with the goal of establishing a collaboratively maintained, machine-readable knowledge base that can be used both in web-based information systems and as semantic knowledge bases in LT applications – ideally, this endeavour should be addressed in a multilingual way on the European scale.

In a number of specific areas of English language research, there already exists software with promising functionality. However, it is clear from our analysis that further research efforts are required to meet the current deficit in processing texts at a deeper semantic level.

4.7 CROSS-LANGUAGE COMPARISON

The current state of LT support varies considerably from one language community to another. In order to compare the situation between languages, this section presents an evaluation based on two sample application areas (machine translation and speech processing) and one underlying technology (text analysis), as well as basic resources needed to construct LT applications. Each language has been categorised using the following five-point scale:

1. Excellent support
2. Good support
3. Moderate support
4. Fragmentary support
5. Weak or no support

Language Technology support was measured according to the following criteria:

Speech Processing: Quality of existing speech recognition technologies, quality of existing speech synthesis technologies, coverage of domains, number and size of existing speech corpora, amount and variety of available speech-based applications.

Machine Translation: Quality of existing MT technologies, number of language pairs covered, coverage of linguistic phenomena and domains, quality and size of existing parallel corpora, amount and variety of available MT applications.

Text Analysis: Quality and coverage of existing text analysis technologies (morphology, syntax, semantics), coverage of linguistic phenomena and domains, amount and variety of available applications, quality and size of existing (annotated) text corpora, quality and coverage of existing lexical resources (e. g., WordNet) and grammars.

Resources: Quality and size of existing text corpora, speech corpora and parallel corpora, quality and coverage of existing lexical resources and grammars.

Figures 9 to 12 (p. 31 and 32) show that, thanks to large-scale LT funding in recent decades, the English language is generally one of the best-equipped languages. However, as can be seen from the above clusters, there is not a single area in which resources for English can be classified as having excellent support. Thus, there are many gaps to be filled with regards to high quality applications for English.

For speech processing, current technologies perform well enough to be successfully integrated into a number of industrial applications, such as spoken dialogue and dictation systems. Today's text analysis components and language resources already cover the linguistic phenomena of English to a certain extent and are integrated into applications that mostly involve shallow natural language processing, e. g., spelling correction and authoring support.

However, for building more sophisticated applications, such as machine translation, there is a clear need for resources and technologies that cover a wider range of linguistic aspects and allow a deep semantic analysis of the input text. By improving the quality and coverage of these basic resources and technologies, we will be able to open up new opportunities for tackling a vast range of advanced application areas, including high-quality machine translation.

4.8 CONCLUSIONS

This series of white papers represents a significant effort, by assessing the language technology support for 30 European languages, and by providing a high-level comparison across these languages. By identifying the gaps, needs and deficits, the European language technology community and its related stakeholders are now in a position to design a large scale research and development programme aimed at building a truly multilingual, technology-enabled communication across Europe.

The results of the analyses reported in this white paper series show that there is a dramatic difference in language technology support between the various European languages. While good quality software and resources are available for some languages and application areas, others, usually smaller languages, have substantial gaps. Many languages lack basic technologies and essential resources for text analysis. Others have basic tools and resources, but the implementation of, for example, semantic methods, is still a long way in the future. Therefore, a large-scale effort is needed to attain the ambitious goal of providing high-quality language technology support for all European languages, for example through accurate machine translation.

It is without doubt that there exist extremely strong foundations on which the already thriving language technology landscape for English can continue to grow and prosper, especially given the well established research communities both in the UK and other English-speaking countries worldwide. However, it is important to emphasise that many aspects of language technology have still yet to be solved. In certain cases, some of these problems concern the need to focus greater research efforts on some of the more complex areas of LT, including advanced discourse processing and language generation. However, some more general issues, including problems of sustainability and adaptability, which are common across many types of tools and resources, are in urgent need of more focussed strategies.

The English language technology industry, dedicated to transforming research into products, is currently fragmented and disorganised. Most large companies have either stopped or severely cut their LT efforts, leaving the field to a number of specialised SMEs that are not robust enough to address both internal and global markets with a sustained strategy.

Our findings show that the only alternative is to make a substantial effort to improve and expand upon the set of LT resources for English, and use them to drive forward research, innovation and development. The need for large amounts of data and the extreme complexity of language technology systems make it vital to develop a new infrastructure and a more coherent research organization, in order to spur greater sharing and cooperation.

The long-term goal of META-NET is to enable the creation of high-quality language technology for all languages. This requires all stakeholders – in politics, research, business and society – to unite their efforts. The resulting technology will help to tear down existing barriers and to build bridges between Europe's languages, thus paving the way for political and economic unity through cultural diversity.

Excellent support	Good support	Moderate support	Fragmentary support	Weak/no support
	English	Czech Dutch Finnish French German Italian Portuguese Spanish	Basque Bulgarian Catalan Danish Estonian Galician Greek Hungarian Irish Norwegian Polish Serbian Slovak Slovene Swedish	Croatian Icelandic Latvian Lithuanian Maltese Romanian

9: Speech processing: state of language technology support for 30 European languages

Excellent support	Good support	Moderate support	Fragmentary support	Weak/no support
	English	French Spanish	Catalan Dutch German Hungarian Italian Polish Romanian	Basque Bulgarian Croatian Czech Danish Estonian Finnish Galician Greek Icelandic Irish Latvian Lithuanian Maltese Norwegian Portuguese Serbian Slovak Slovene Swedish

10: Machine translation: state of language technology support for 30 European languages

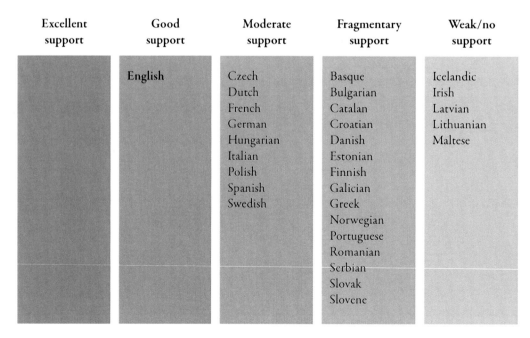

Excellent support	Good support	Moderate support	Fragmentary support	Weak/no support
	English	Dutch	Basque	Croatian
		French	Bulgarian	Estonian
		German	Catalan	Icelandic
		Italian	Czech	Irish
		Spanish	Danish	Latvian
			Finnish	Lithuanian
			Galician	Maltese
			Greek	Serbian
			Hungarian	
			Norwegian	
			Polish	
			Portuguese	
			Romanian	
			Slovak	
			Slovene	
			Swedish	

11: Text analysis: state of language technology support for 30 European languages

Excellent support	Good support	Moderate support	Fragmentary support	Weak/no support
	English	Czech	Basque	Icelandic
		Dutch	Bulgarian	Irish
		French	Catalan	Latvian
		German	Croatian	Lithuanian
		Hungarian	Danish	Maltese
		Italian	Estonian	
		Polish	Finnish	
		Spanish	Galician	
		Swedish	Greek	
			Norwegian	
			Portuguese	
			Romanian	
			Serbian	
			Slovak	
			Slovene	

12: Speech and text resources: State of support for 30 European languages

5

ABOUT META-NET

META-NET is a Network of Excellence funded by the European Commission [43]. The network currently consists of 54 members in 33 European countries. META-NET forges **META**, the Multilingual Europe Technology Alliance, a growing community of language technology professionals and organisations in Europe. META-NET fosters the technological foundations for a truly multilingual European information society that:

- makes communication and cooperation possible across languages;
- grants all Europeans equal access to information and knowledge regardless of their language;
- builds upon and advances functionalities of networked information technology.

The network supports a Europe that unites as a single digital market and information space. It stimulates and promotes multilingual technologies for all European languages. These technologies support automatic translation, content production, information processing and knowledge management for a wide variety of subject domains and applications. They also enable intuitive language-based interfaces to technology ranging from household electronics, machinery and vehicles to computers and robots.

Launched on 1 February 2010, META-NET has already conducted various activities in its three lines of action META-VISION, META-SHARE and META-RESEARCH.

META-VISION fosters a dynamic and influential stakeholder community that unites around a shared vision and a common strategic research agenda (SRA). The main focus of this activity is to build a coherent and cohesive LT community in Europe by bringing together representatives from highly fragmented and diverse groups of stakeholders. The present white paper was prepared together with volumes for 29 other languages. The shared technology vision was developed in three sectorial Vision Groups. The META Technology Council was established in order to discuss and to prepare the SRA based on the vision in close interaction with the entire LT community.

META-SHARE creates an open, distributed facility for exchanging and sharing resources. The peer-to-peer network of repositories will contain language data, tools and web services that are documented with high-quality metadata and organised in standardised categories. The resources can be readily accessed and uniformly searched. The available resources include free, open source materials as well as restricted, commercially available, fee-based items.

META-RESEARCH builds bridges to related technology fields. This activity seeks to leverage advances in other fields and to capitalise on innovative research that can benefit language technology. In particular, the action line focusses on conducting leading-edge research in machine translation, collecting data, preparing data sets and organising language resources for evaluation purposes; compiling inventories of tools and methods; and organising workshops and training events for members of the community.

office@meta-net.eu – http://www.meta-net.eu

≡A

REFERENCES

[1] Aljoscha Burchardt, Markus Egg, Kathrin Eichler, Brigitte Krenn, Jörn Kreutel, Annette Leßmöllmann, Georg Rehm, Manfred Stede, Hans Uszkoreit, and Martin Volk. *Die Deutsche Sprache im Digitalen Zeitalter – The German Language in the Digital Age*. META-NET White Paper Series. Georg Rehm and Hans Uszkoreit (Series Editors). Springer, 2012.

[2] Aljoscha Burchardt, Georg Rehm, and Felix Sasaki. The Future European Multilingual Information Society – Vision Paper for a Strategic Research Agenda, 2011. http://www.meta-net.eu/vision/reports/meta-net-vision-paper.pdf.

[3] Directorate-General Information Society & Media of the European Commission. User Language Preferences Online, 2011. http://ec.europa.eu/public_opinion/flash/fl_313_en.pdf.

[4] European Commission. Multilingualism: an Asset for Europe and a Shared Commitment, 2008. http://ec.europa.eu/languages/pdf/comm2008_en.pdf.

[5] Directorate-General of the UNESCO. Intersectoral Mid-term Strategy on Languages and Multilingualism, 2007. http://unesdoc.unesco.org/images/0015/001503/150335e.pdf.

[6] Directorate-General for Translation of the European Commission. Size of the Language Industry in the EU, 2009. http://ec.europa.eu/dgs/translation/publications/studies.

[7] European Federation of National Institutions for Language. Language Legislation in the United Kingdom. http://www.efnil.org/documents/language-legislation-version-2007/united-kingdom/english.

[8] The National Archives. Welsh Language (Wales) Measure 2011. http://www.legislation.gov.uk/mwa/2011/1/section/1/enacted, 2011.

[9] David Crystal. *The English Language: A Guided Tour of the Language*. Penguin, 2002.

[10] David Crystal. *Evolving English: One Language, Many Voices*. The British Library Publishing Division, 2010.

[11] Melvyn Bragg. *The Adventure of English*. Sceptre, 2004.

[12] Bill Bryson. *Mother Tongue: The Story of the English Language*. Penguin, 2009.

[13] Frank C. Laubach. *Let's Reform Spelling – Why and How*. Nre Readers Press, NY, 1996.

[14] Oxford English Dictionary. OED March 2011 update. http://www.oed.com/public/update0311, 2011.

[15] Eurobarometer. Europeans and their Languages. http://ec.europa.eu/public_opinion/archives/ebs/ebs_243_sum_en.pdf, 2006.

[16] The University of Leicester. The English Association. http://www.le.ac.uk/engassoc/.

[17] Council for College and University English. http://www.ccue.ac.uk.

[18] National Association for the Teaching of English. http://www.nate.org.uk.

[19] The European Society for the Study of English. http://www.essenglish.org.

[20] The Queen's English Society. http://www.queens-english-society.com.

[21] Department for Education, Employment & Qualifications, and Curriculum Authority. The National Curriculum for England: Key Stages 1-4. http://www.education.gov.uk/curriculum, 1999.

[22] Joanne L. Emery. Uptake of GCE A-level subjects in England 2006. http://www.cambridgeassessment.org.uk/ca/digitalAssets/113995_Stats_report_5_-_A_level_uptake_2006.pdf, 2007.

[23] OECD. OECD Programme for International Student Assessment (PISA). http://www.pisa.oecd.org.

[24] Eurydice Network. Key Data on Teaching Languages at School in Europe. http://eacea.ec.europa.eu/about/eurydice/documents/KDL2008_EN.pdf, 2008.

[25] John M. Swales. English as Tyrannosaurus Rex. *World Englishes*, pages 373–382, 1997.

[26] Office for National Statistics. Internet Access 2010: Households and Individuals. http://www.ons.gov.uk/ons/rel/rdit2/internet-access---households-and-individuals/2010/stb-internet-access---households-and-individuals--2010.pdf, 2010.

[27] Internet World Stats. Internet World Users By Language: Top 10 Languages. http://www.internetworldstats.com/stats7.htm, 2010.

[28] DENIC. Domainzahlenvergleich international (Comparison figures for international domains). http://www.denic.de/hintergrund/statistiken/internationale-domainstatistik.html, 2010.

[29] Daniel Jurafsky and James H. Martin. *Speech and Language Processing*. Prentice Hall, 2 edition, 2009.

[30] Christopher D. Manning and Hinrich Schütze. *Foundations of Statistical Natural Language Processing*. MIT Press, 1999.

[31] Language Technology World (LT World). http://www.lt-world.org.

[32] Ronald Cole, Joseph Mariani, Hans Uszkoreit, Giovanni Battista Varile, Annie Zaenen, and Antonio Zampolli, editors. *Survey of the State of the Art in Human Language Technology*. Cambridge University Press, 1998.

[33] Jerrold H. Zar. Candidate for a Pullet Surprise. *Journal of Irreproducible Results*, page 13, 1994.

[34] Aerospace & Defence Association of Europe. ASD Simplified Technical English Maintenance Group (STEMG). http://www.asd-ste100.org.

[35] Tedopres International. HyperSTE Software. http://www.simplifiedenglish.net/HyperSTE-Software/.

[36] StatCounter. Top 5 Search Engines in United Kindgdom from Oct to Dec 2010. http://gs.statcounter.com/#search_engine-GB-monthly-201010-201012, 2010.

[37] Juan Carlos Perez. Google Rolls out Semantic Search Capabilities, 2009. http://www.pcworld.com/businesscenter/article/161869/google_rolls_out_semantic_search_capabilities.html.

[38] Peter M. Kruse, André Naujoks, Dietmar Rösner, and Manuela Kunze. Clever Search: A WordNet Based Wrapper for Internet Search Engines. In *Proceedings of GLDV Tagung*, 2005.

[39] Mike Cohen. Can we talk? Better Speech Technology with Phonectic Arts. http://googleblog.blogspot.com/2010/12/can-we-talk-better-speech-technology.html, 2010.

[40] University of Edinburgh Centre for Speech Technology. The Festival Speech Synthesis System. http://www.cstr.ed.ac.uk/projects/festival/.

[41] Philipp Koehn, Alexandra Birch, and Ralf Steinberger. 462 Machine Translation Systems for Europe. In *Proceedings of MT Summit XII*, 2009.

[42] Kishore Papineni, Salim Roukos, Todd Ward, and Wei-Jing Zhu. BLEU: A Method for Automatic Evaluation of Machine Translation. In *Proceedings of the 40th Annual Meeting of ACL*, Philadelphia, PA, 2002.

[43] Georg Rehm and Hans Uszkoreit. Multilingual Europe: A challenge for language tech. *MultiLingual*, 22(3):51–52, April/May 2011.

META-NET MEMBERS

Austria	Zentrum für Translationswissenschaft, Universität Wien: Gerhard Budin
Belgium	Centre for Processing Speech and Images, University of Leuven: Dirk van Compernolle
	Computational Linguistics and Psycholinguistics Research Centre, University of Antwerp: Walter Daelemans
Bulgaria	Institute for Bulgarian Language, Bulgarian Academy of Sciences: Svetla Koeva
Croatia	Institute of Linguistics, Faculty of Humanities and Social Science, University of Zagreb: Marko Tadić
Cyprus	Language Centre, School of Humanities: Jack Burston
Czech Republic	Institute of Formal and Applied Linguistics, Charles University in Prague: Jan Hajič
Denmark	Centre for Language Technology, University of Copenhagen: Bolette Sandford Pedersen, Bente Maegaard
Estonia	Institute of Computer Science, University of Tartu: Tiit Roosmaa, Kadri Vider
Finland	Computational Cognitive Systems Research Group, Aalto University: Timo Honkela
	Department of Modern Languages, University of Helsinki: Kimmo Koskenniemi, Krister Lindén
France	Centre National de la Recherche Scientifique, Laboratoire d'Informatique pour la Mécanique et les Sciences de l'Ingénieur and Institute for Multilingual and Multimedia Information: Joseph Mariani
	Evaluations and Language Resources Distribution Agency: Khalid Choukri
Germany	Language Technology Lab, DFKI: Hans Uszkoreit, Georg Rehm
	Human Language Technology and Pattern Recognition, RWTH Aachen University: Hermann Ney
	Department of Computational Linguistics, Saarland University: Manfred Pinkal
Greece	R.C. "Athena", Institute for Language and Speech Processing: Stelios Piperidis
Hungary	Research Institute for Linguistics, Hungarian Academy of Sciences: Tamás Váradi
	Department of Telecommunications and Media Informatics, Budapest University of Technology and Economics: Géza Németh, Gábor Olaszy
Iceland	School of Humanities, University of Iceland: Eiríkur Rögnvaldsson
Ireland	School of Computing, Dublin City University: Josef van Genabith
Italy	Consiglio Nazionale delle Ricerche, Istituto di Linguistica Computazionale "Antonio Zampolli": Nicoletta Calzolari
	Human Language Technology Research Unit, Fondazione Bruno Kessler: Bernardo Magnini

Latvia	Tilde: Andrejs Vasiļjevs
	Institute of Mathematics and Computer Science, University of Latvia: Inguna Skadiņa
Lithuania	Institute of the Lithuanian Language: Jolanta Zabarskaitė
Luxembourg	Arax Ltd.: Vartkes Goetcherian
Malta	Department Intelligent Computer Systems, University of Malta: Mike Rosner
Netherlands	Utrecht Institute of Linguistics, Utrecht University: Jan Odijk
	Computational Linguistics, University of Groningen: Gertjan van Noord
Norway	Department of Linguistic, Literary and Aesthetic Studies, University of Bergen: Koenraad De Smedt
	Department of Informatics, Language Technology Group, University of Oslo: Stephan Oepen
Poland	Institute of Computer Science, Polish Academy of Sciences: Adam Przepiórkowski, Maciej Ogrodniczuk
	University of Łódź: Barbara Lewandowska-Tomaszczyk, Piotr Pęzik
	Dept. of Comp. Linguistics and Artificial Intelligence, Adam Mickiewicz University: Zygmunt Vetulani
Portugal	University of Lisbon: António Branco, Amália Mendes
	Spoken Language Systems Laboratory, Institute for Systems Engineering and Computers: Isabel Trancoso
Romania	Faculty of Computer Science, University Alexandru Ioan Cuza of Iași: Dan Cristea
	Research Institute for Artificial Intelligence, Romanian Academy of Sciences: Dan Tufiș
Serbia	University of Belgrade, Faculty of Mathematics: Duško Vitas, Cvetana Krstev, Ivan Obradović
	Pupin Institute: Sanja Vranes
Slovakia	Ľudovít Štúr Institute of Linguistics, Slovak Academy of Sciences: Radovan Garabík
Slovenia	Jožef Stefan Institute: Marko Grobelnik
Spain	Barcelona Media: Toni Badia, Maite Melero
	Aholab Signal Processing Laboratory, University of the Basque Country: Inma Hernaez Rioja
	Center for Language and Speech Technologies and Applications, Universitat Politècnica de Catalunya: Asunción Moreno
	Department of Signal Processing and Communications, University of Vigo: Carmen García Mateo
	Institut Universitari de Lingüística Aplicada, Universitat Pompeu Fabra: Núria Bel
Sweden	Department of Swedish, University of Gothenburg: Lars Borin
Switzerland	Idiap Research Institute: Hervé Bourlard
UK	School of Computer Science, University of Manchester: Sophia Ananiadou
	Institute for Language, Cognition and Computation, Center for Speech Technology Research, University of Edinburgh: Steve Renals
	Research Institute of Informatics and Language Processing, University of Wolverhampton: Ruslan Mitkov

About 100 language technology experts – representatives of the countries and languages represented in META-NET – discussed and finalised the key results and messages of the White Paper Series at a META-NET meeting in Berlin, Germany, on October 21/22, 2011.

THE META-NET WHITE PAPER SERIES

Basque	euskara
Bulgarian	български
Catalan	català
Croatian	hrvatski
Czech	čeština
Danish	dansk
Dutch	Nederlands
English	English
Estonian	eesti
Finnish	suomi
French	français
Galician	galego
German	Deutsch
Greek	ελληνικά
Hungarian	magyar
Icelandic	íslenska
Irish	Gaeilge
Italian	italiano
Latvian	latviešu valoda
Lithuanian	lietuvių kalba
Maltese	Malti
Norwegian Bokmål	bokmål
Norwegian Nynorsk	nynorsk
Polish	polski
Portuguese	português
Romanian	română
Serbian	српски
Slovak	slovenčina
Slovene	slovenščina
Spanish	español
Swedish	svenska